A3D Impressions™

A division of Awareness 3D LLC
PO Box 57415
Tucson, Arizona USA 85732
www.a3dimpressions.com

Copyright © 2018 by Embody Learning LLC

All rights reserved, including the right to reproduce this book or portions thereof in any form whatsoever without permission. Contact A3D Impressions Rights & Permission.

First A3D Impressions Edition 2018

design: Donn Poll

ISBN 978-1-7320677-8-3
LCCN 2018936823

1 2 3 4 5 6 7 8 9 10

EMBODY LEARNING®

STUDENT ENGAGEMENT GUIDE

Julia Barwell
Donn Poll
Rick Wamer

CONTRIBUTORS

J. David Betts Eric Nelson
Jean Cole Cheryl Mertz
Dina Delaney Melissa Shaver
Paul Fisher Jessica Summers

© 2018 Embody Learning LLC

5352 Bloomington Avenue
Minneapolis, Minnesota USA 55417

embodylearning.com

EMBODY LEARNING

STUDENT ENGAGEMENT GUIDE

	For Teachers Who Do their Best 6
	Tips for Using this Guide 8
1	EXAMINE THE EMBODY LEARNING MODEL 10
	Embody Learning Classrooms 11
	Why Embody Learning? 13
	Does it Work? 15
	The Practice 16
	Familiar Theoretical Grounding 18
2	TOTAL COMMITMENT LEARNING 22
	Four Aspects of How Students Learn 23
3	SKILLS THAT DRIVE THE MODEL 26
	Collaboration 28
	Presentation 46
	Innovation 60
	Improvisation 72
4	LESSON PLANNING 82
	STEP 1: New Lens on Content 84
	Inherent Opportunities 86
	Relevance 88
	The Senses 94
	Students Can Own Their Learning 96
	STEP 2: Put Action in the Lesson 98
	Engage 100
	Explore 102
	Show 104
5	BUILD AN EMBODY LEARNING ENVIRONMENT 106
	What Teachers Say 110
	Appendix 111

For

Teachers

who do their best to engage every student in their classrooms...

...have a commitment to continually grow and improve, using experience to build knowledge...

...who are constantly looking for ways to improve their teaching practice — for techniques, methods, tools, examples of breakthroughs that are more than just the next trend...

If you are that teacher... this is your guide. It's about a teaching mode developed by visionary teachers taking bold steps to engage every student in their classrooms, creating active learning experiences every day.

They start with a model but do it their own way. And you can do it your way. Here's how.

First, let's agree that teachers — you — more than public policy, more than education budgets, more than any other group or single person, are in the best position to have an impact on the success of every student in your classroom.

Your impact is not so much about what you teach.

Your opportunity to engage every student is in how you teach.

Your success as a teacher is about the learning experiences you create each day.

Definition

Embody Learning is a method of teaching that equips teachers to actively engage every learner in total commitment learning.

A pedagogy — the practice of teaching — especially as an academic subject or theoretical concept.

Student engagement is the degree of attention, curiosity, interest, optimism and passion that students show when they are learning.

Learning that engages each student individual physically, emotionally, intellectually and socially.

tips for using this guide

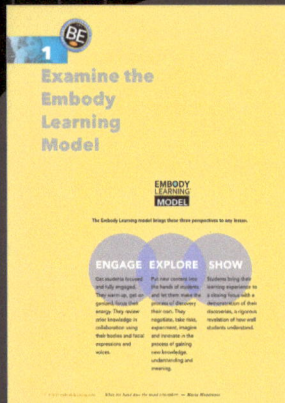

To learn about the Embody Learning model and how it works, including data on its effectiveness and academic grounding, start with sections 1 and 2 beginning on **page 14**.

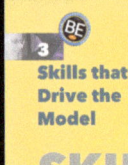

To gain skills that support the classroom practice of Embody Learning, go to **page 26**.

Find examples of Embody Learning in the classroom in the yellow boxes.

For the strategic view of your classroom practice, refer often to **page 106**.

To get right to the practice of Embody Learning in lesson planning and student engagement in your classroom, open your guide to **page 82**.

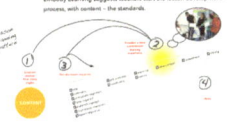

9

1
Examine the Embody Learning Model

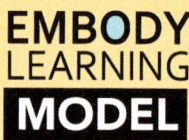

The Embody Learning model brings these three perspectives to any lesson.

ENGAGE
Get students focused and fully engaged. They warm up, get organized, focus their energy. They review prior knowledge in collaboration using their bodies and facial expressions and voices.

EXPLORE
Put new content into the hands of students and let them make the process of discovery their own. They negotiate, take risks, experiment, imagine and innovate in the process of gaining new knowledge, understanding and meaning.

SHOW
Students bring their learning experience to a closing focus with a demonstration of their discoveries, a rigorous revelation of how well students understand.

What the hand does the mind remembers. — *Maria Montessori*

Embody Learning in classrooms

"When converting a mixed number to an improper fraction, students used the desk as the fraction line. As the whole number moved to multiply themselves by the denominator, they moved on top of the table to add to the numerator and create an equivalent improper fraction. When asked to explain how to convert mixed numbers into improper fractions, students went so far as to draw pictures of students going through that process. Overall, I noticed an incredible increase in not only vocabulary retention and test scores, but most importantly the students took ownership of the words and processes and the level of enjoyment they had with the vocabulary lessons. In our final Embody Learning lesson, students showed truly how far they had come when they were able to perform and compare their vocabulary words so that students were able to understand the differences between quadrilaterals."

- fifth grade teacher

Student fully engaged in exploring knowledge and demonsrating the learning process.

©2018 embodylearning.com

1 Examine the Embody Learning Model

In their seats vs. on their feet

If you walked into a conventional classroom and asked students to demonstrate their learning, they could be a little self-conscious or they might start in on a long verbal exposition.

In an Embody Learning environment, where students have learned through intellectual, physical, emotional, and social engagement, students will get on their feet, come together and repeat one of many knowledge demonstrations. It's a revelation, and it could be a revolution.

Embody Learning lessons include demonstrations of learning by students, often in groups, of new knowledge before the full class.

Teachers new to Embody Learning are consistently surprised at the volume of content displayed in the demonstration phase of Embody Learning lessons — surprised that even struggling students are exceeding expectations as all students participate fully.

The future belongs to a very different kind of person with a very different kind of mind - creators and

Why Embody Learning?

Because we all learn by experience. Embody Learning makes every lesson a learning experience.

==For teachers:==

Embody Learning is a tool for lesson planning. Planning an Embody Learning lesson is defining how content can be *experienced* by students.

Embody Learning is a pedagogy — a guide for how you teach. In the classroom, Embody Learning is how teachers connect with every student in the classroom. Classroom management becomes a side issue as students discover the joy of giving their whole selves to active learning.

==For students:==

Embody Learning is a guaranteed effective learning experience. It goes beyond seeing and hearing. Embody Learning is learning with their bodies, emotions, relationships with other students, other senses, and their curiosity, aspirations, passions and discoveries. It's how they want to learn every day.

So why Embody Learning? Because it invites everyone to bring their full selves to the learning field and lets them relish the sense that they can discover as much as they are willing to pursue.

emphasizers, pattern recognizers and meaning makers. — Daniel H. Pink

1 Examine the Embody Learning Model

Teachers find that the Embody Learning model opens a well- stocked toolbox. The model supports the full range of learning and teaching modalities — supporting a multimodal classroom. Its tools complement any teacher's strengths — passions, experience, talents and aspirations — and offer compensation for weaknesses that the best teachers learn to work around.

Embody Learning lessons enable teachers to build on their best ideas, and their best attributes: optimism, insight, attention to detail, a gift for seeing the big picture, persistence, patience, a sense of design, fairness, courage… you get the idea. The working theory is that teachers will move students into trying new learning modalities and that students will be engaged and support the new ideas and collaborate in their success. While that may sound idealistic, it plays out realistically time after time.

Embody Learning addresses HOW content is presented, not WHAT content is presented. That means any content, any curriculum or standards, can be a fit with the model. Whether a school uses the Common Core State Standards or other standards, a specific curriculum package or program, or is a public, private, charter or even home school, a teacher can empower students to embody the content.

Elementary students embody a verb in an English lesson.

Stop thinking schoolishly. Stop acting teacherishly. Stop talking about learning as though it's separate

Does it work?

When we examine evidence from classrooms in which teachers are using Embody Learning to teach core content, there is a consistent correlation between its practice and student success. In every school in which we measured student achievement, test scores increased. In one grade 5 and 6 study of Embody Learning classes, teachers using Embody Learning increased test scores by

- 42% in math
- 54% in social studies
- 60% in science.

Grades increase because:
- Students own their learning.
- Collaboration allows students to build their own understanding of content.
- Students discover the relevance of content.
- Students and teachers push past barriers and focus on the experience of exploration, discovery, creativity, and accomplishment.

Teachers report that a higher level of student engagement reduces classroom management issues. Students with social or behavioral issues find active learning creates an environment in which they can participate more fully with their peers. Students gain a new level of engagement with learning. Student attitudes about school shift and parents notice. (See embodylearning.com for more data.)

from life. — Sandra Dodd

1 Examine the Embody Learning Model

The Practice

Embody Learning is a methodology — a pedagogy — of teaching. It has a focus on strategies and a set of skills.

It is similar to several instructional methods: active learning, embodied learning, simulation learning, project-based learning, social and emotional learning (SEL), and others. Like Embody Learning, these engage students in some form of multi-sensory activities in the learning process.

Embody Learning grew out of arts integration, which used the arts as vehicles for learning academic subjects. In the case of Embody Learning, the arts used to define the active engagement component of every lesson. Eventually, the arts gave way to academic content as the dominant priority. Now, in the Embody Learning process, content defines the active engagement strategy for each lesson.

A New Level of Teaching and Learning

The Embody Learning pedagogy calls on a new level of teaching and learning: total commitment teaching and learning. That means all the human faculties are called to the task.

Students no longer sit in seats facing the front like in a Norman Rockwell painting of a classroom. Desks, if there are any, are pushed back and students will be working in groups, physically exploring content in mathematics or science or language.

No one is born fully-formed: it is through self-experience in the world that we become what we are.

This is the picture of a classroom where students discover their own joy of learning. Many teachers already use a teaching style similar to Embody Learning for some lessons, occasionally, for a project or when the content easily translates into an active lesson. Most likely, students love it and results show it.

Embody Learning is designed to be a **day-to-day practice** that extends the positive results of active learning to more, if not all, lessons. The pedagogy is especially effective in equalizing the learning experience across a diverse class of students and raising performance among at-risk students. According to research done by the Program for International Student Assessment (PISA), many US students are behind students from other countries in their achievement in math, science, and literacy. This is especially true among students of color, students with disabilities, and English learners who consistently have less access to full academic offerings in their schools (USDE Office of Civil Rights). Embody Learning excels within these populations.

While the teacher's role in education matters more than any other aspect of schooling (Rand, 2016), neither preservice nor in-service professional development provides adequate pedagogical support, let alone a dynamic set of skills and technical support required to help teachers meet the needs of a challenged student population (MDR/EdNET, 2016).

High school students embodying the solution to a quadratic equation.

Early learners practicing learning skills in preparation for math and language learning.

— *Paulo Freire*

1
Examine
the Embody
Learning
Model

Standing on Familiar Theoretical Grounding

The basis for Embody Learning is constructivist learning theory as elaborated by John Dewey, Jean Piaget, Jerome Bruner, Lev Vygotsky, and others, and Albert Bandura's social learning theory, which suggests that people can learn though observation, including direct instruction, modeling, and imitation. "The highest level of observational learning," Bandura argues (1977) "is achieved by first organizing and rehearsing the modeled behavior symbolically and then enacting it overtly."

David H. Jonassen (2002) describes a constructivist learning environment as a classroom model. Learners interact with real objects and real problems, and — with coaching and reference support — construct their own knowledge.

The Embody Learning model emphasizes making all learning active and an embodiment of content. As the model has developed since 2012, teachers have developed Embody Learning in schools with a range of student populations — schools with low income populations and in middle class neighborhoods, 100 percent bilingual schools, Native American schools, charter schools, parochial schools, arts schools, diverse urban high schools, rural K-8 schools, private and public preschools.

Embody Learning as a methodology offers support to teachers as they learn to incorporate the whole learner in tangible experiences related to curriculum content goals. Recognizing that even the most eloquent lectures cannot create a tactile experience, Embody Learning helps teachers build student-focused lessons.

Bandura, A., & Walters, R. H. (1977). *Social Learning Theory.*

Jonassen, D. H. (2002). Learning as activity. *Educational Technology,* 42(2), 45-51.

That path to understanding in the Embody Learning model acknowledges the multi-dimensional nature of learners. Play, art and active learning are all related to developmental processes that we experience throughout our lives (Bredikyte, 2010). Play is an expression of the child's developing personality and is essential for optimal development and learning in young children (Vygotsky, 1976). A real object in a play situation allows the child to make a move in the field of senses, which leads to mastering the meaning of the object of reference in the future (Goffman, E. 1959). Taken together, these dimensions of learning define the need for lessons that engage students holistically. Lessons that guide students to embody content and meaning achieve holistic — total — engagement with students.

Bending, twisting, reaching, turning, and shifting energy through movement, seventh graders at an urban Phoenix middle school were embodying chemical reactions in science class. They worked in small groups using their bodies to convey specific properties of one of five chemical reactions. Each group developed a set of movements and showed it to their classmates, who looked for the specific content of their presentations. The onlookers identified the content of the science and named which of the five chemical reactions the acting group was conveying in their presentation. Students were prompted to critique, fine tune, and adjust each other's representations. Every student participated, shy and outgoing, A-students and barely passing students.

The teacher noted that having her students build scientific concepts with their bodies allowed her to assess their understanding of chemical reactions. The collaborative environment that had encouraged students to build social skills nurtured problem solving. Many second language English speakers in this classroom were focused and engaged throughout the lesson. Key vocabulary became vividly embodied in the model of learning so that all students, including ELL students, shared a clear understanding of critical science content. The evidence of this understanding showed up in diagrams that students created later.

Bredikyte, M. (2010). Psychological tools and the development of play. *Cultural-Historical Psychology*, (4).

Vygotsky, L. S. (1976). Play and its role in the mental development of the child.

Goffman, E. (1959). The Presentation of Self in. *Butler, Bodies that Matter.*

1 Examine the Embody Learning Model

Play is a critical learning skill, just as play is how we learn at the beginning of life and becomes a permanent part of everyday life. As Lawrence Pearsall Jacks wrote in *Education through Recreation*: "A master in the art of living makes little distinction between his work and his play, his labor and his leisure, his mind and his body..."

Like play, the arts are the source of learning. The incorporation of arts-derived activities in the classroom can serve as a powerful tool for helping teachers translate findings from neuroscience and cognitive science into instructional practice (Hardiman, 2010). The benefits for content learning have been identified across the curriculum (Rinne, et al, 2011; Salomon & Perkins, 1998).

Play and the arts lead to games and puzzles. While technology wants to enter the classroom with video games, a better solution is to develop Embody Learning lessons that use gaming and puzzle formats to engage students.

Embody Learning is infused with play, physical movement, modeling, the arts, and an approach to learning that ramps up to entrepreneurship and STEM careers. Students are learning to guide their own learning, as an entrepreneur will need to invent their business and career or a worker in technology or science will need to make creative and technical breakthroughs. Unlike outdated pedagogies, Embody Learning is how the real world works outside of the classroom.

Hardiman, M. M. (2010). The creative-artistic brain. *Mind, brain, and education: Neuroscience implications for the classroom*, 226-246.

Bäckman, L., Nyberg, L., Soveri, A., Johansson, J., Andersson, M., Dahlin, E., ... & Rinne, J. O. (2011). Effects of working-memory training on striatal dopamine release. Science, 333(6043), 718-718.

Salomon, G., & Perkins, D. N. (1998). Chapter 1: Individual and social aspects of learning. *Review of research in education*, 23(1), 1-24.

At a small rural school in central Arizona, 28 kindergarten students imagine they are seeds growing into plants. They use their bodies to represent the seed pushing through the soil, growing, swaying in the wind, feeling the rain on their leaves, flowering, going to seed, tumbling off the wind to be re-planted as seeds and begin in the life cycle again.

They narrate the various steps and demonstrate their vocabulary. They imagine plants by naming flowers and creating variety. During the process they collaborate to explore environmental variables that impact their growth. Students share leadership, tap prior knowledge, negotiate conclusions and fully include each of their classmates in the process for 30 minutes. When they are done, the children spontaneously cheer for more. They have fun. They learn. They remember. They look forward to school the next day and to another learning experience.

Their teacher observes and participates. She evaluates her students' understanding of the life cycle of a seed, building on the experience with new science vocabulary and using movement as a vehicle for internalizing the cycle and each of its elements. Children are invited to give input and innovate on the spot to extend their learning. The entire process serves as a vehicle for assessment, active engagement, and problem solving for the kindergarten students and their teacher.

When children are given the opportunity to learn in the multi-modal kinesthetic mode that is natural to them, the learning becomes relevant knowledge they can apply outside the classroom as well as recall in their classroom.

2
Total Commitment Learning

CONNECT

act
physic

in

A well-known line in E.M. Forster's novel *Howard's End*, "Only Connect" could be the mantra for teaching. Of course, it's more detailed than the word *only* would suggest.

Connecting content on multiple levels can make the difference between success and failure for any student. To be emotionally stirred, socially supported, with physical expressions of content and intellectual insights — those connections spark powerful moments of learning.

We call it total commitment learning, the Embody Learning definition of connecting on many levels.

feel
emotional

total commitment learning

social
interact

llectual
think

©2018 embodylearning.com

2
Total Commitment Learning

Key to getting full commitment during a lesson is to connect on multiple levels. We have identified four levels that cover lots of ground: intellectual, physical, emotional and social. You achieve total commitment learning when you engage students on these levels.

Students have lots of energy in each of these areas but have not necessarily had it focused on learning in the classroom. That's the opportunity for teachers — to provide and guide the focus.

What does a classroom of total commitment learning look like? It might look like all students huddled together working out a plan, or in groups noisily negotiating various solutions to a math, English or social studies problem. Or a class of early learning students are on their feet following the teacher counting or learning the alphabet. Or seniors working in pairs to prepare presentations to their peers showing what happens when two elements on the periodic table come together.

On the next page is a brief overview of total commitment learning for teachers and students.

Education is an act of love, and thus an act of courage. — *Paulo Freire*

Total commitment considers four aspects of how students learn:

For teachers	For students
Intellectual • Focus on key words and phrases from content. • Ask pithy questions. • Invite participation from everyone. • Use clear statements of content. • State problem and suggest how to pursue answers/solutions together. • Encourage critical thinking: negotiating, idea generating, planning, analysis, evaluation.	Think, problem solve, retrieve existing knowledge, reason, rationalize and put together meaning from new data you acquire through experience and direct delivery from the teacher and peers, materials, media.
Physical • Design the lesson for students to use their bodies to discover meaning and understanding from content. • Consider physical aspects of emotional, social and intellectual expression. • Use facial expressions effectively.	BE the content. Be the learning and use physical action to embody meaning and understanding.
Emotional • Develop understanding of emotion as integrated part of all learning. • Derive emotional aspect of all content. Incorporate it into every lesson plan.	Consider the emotional aspect of content and its impact on you as learner.
Social • Develop a sense of individual students functioning in a group and the group as an entity. • Create an awareness of the impact (and skills) of interactions with peers and adults. • Establish social protocols or patterns for engaging with peers in the act of connecting with content in a learning experience (speaking, listening, empathy, focus, accomplishment, learning).	Engage with peers in a learning process: Asking questions, persuading, offering ideas and listening and building cooperation as you build a learning relationship among your peers. This is not only about a person learning in a classroom. It is about a group of persons learning together.

3

Skills that Drive the Model

SKILLS

Talent, experience, passion, a drive to help students succeed and other human capital are what teachers bring to their daily classroom tasks. These are deeply personal qualities and require time to cultivate. But skills — capacities that can be acquired through practice, training and acquisition of knowledge — are accessible in a short time by teachers who make a commitment to pursue them with diligence. You couldn't decide to acquire a talent for music, but you could certainly decide to learn a skill of playing a guitar.

We've identified a set of skills that invigorate the use of Embody Learning: presentation, collaboration, innovation and improvisation. A couple are general teaching skills while others are slightly outside the traditional teaching box. You get the benefits as you use these skills in your daily teaching practice and your students learn them too.

3
Skills
that Drive
the Model

Collaboration

Students today need to learn two important things from school: how to face uncertainty, and how to

The benefits of working together are numerous. A group has more ideas than an individual. A group provides immediate feedback on ideas. A group offers discussion of strategy — and problem solving — from different perspectives. A group can overcome social barriers so that everyone participates equally.

Research has documented the superior performance of teams over individuals working alone (Ladley 2015). While K-12 teaching is often called an isolated profession, research on collaborative projects has demonstrated measurable success. Collaborative learning means that students see themselves as a group — a class or subgroups within — and that they work using the teacher's guidance but without constant instruction.

Learning in collaboration enables each participant to be a teacher and a learner, an inquirer and a discoverer. Within collaboration, we explore trust, share participation, pick up common attitudes, and develop a standard for communication.

> *In the long history of humankind ... those who learned to collaborate and improvise most effectively have prevailed.*
> *- Charles Darwin*

Ladley, D., Wilkinson, I., & Young, L. (2015). The impact of individual versus group rewards on work group performance and cooperation: A computational social science approach. *Journal of Business Research, 68*(11), 2412-2425.

SKILLS: Collaboration

Trust

Relationships count

WHY: The better you know someone, the easier it is to trust them. Many conferences and trainings start with a warm-up exercise in which participants exchange personal information. Such an exchange creates references that people use to connect with each other throughout the event that might even start a professional friendship. Embody Learning will have students working closely together every day. Trust will build and the learning environment will grow stronger.

HOW: Plan — Put a trust-building activity on the agenda or in the lesson. (try this one: https://tomprof.stanford.edu/posting/1611). The simple act of being part of a group builds relationships — sharing information about our background, using talents and skills, volunteering to assume a role, even asking for help. Use a go-around introduction at your next meeting to get some piece of personal information from each participant — like the last book or movie participants experienced that links to their work. For students, ask for information that builds trust, breaks down barriers, and links to content.

SKILLS: Collaboration
Trust

Optimize feedback

WHY: For teachers, feedback is essential to continually improving classroom practice. For students, learning to give and receive feedback in a constructive fashion is a valuable learning skill.

HOW: Ask to be observed teaching an Embody Learning lesson, with notes. Videotape your teaching and review with a colleague or coach. Run ideas by colleagues, including concepts, materials, and outlines. With students, pair up and practice a feedback exchange on a lesson-related process. Follow with a general discussion of what helps and what doesn't. Discuss issues with students learning to receive and give constructive feedback.

Skills that Drive the Model

SKILLS: Collaboration

Trust

Consider empathy

WHY: You have to admit that the wolf who ate Red Riding-hood's grandmother must have been hungry. Is that admission empathy? Everyone has a viewpoint and some motivation. Empathy could help us see individuals clearly if we can pull it off without prejudice, which is important for the role of teacher and students in collaboration.

HOW: Teach students to pause long enough to make an effort to understand the circumstance — and the viewpoint — of other people on the team. Do not assume another person's viewpoint. Listen. Share any feelings another person shares with you. Attempt to gain an understanding of their circumstances. For example, a new student will share the experience of what it is like to be a new student. A non-English speaker might do the same about being an ELL student. You and other students can show empathy. Apply the old adage: Walk a mile in her shoes.

All learning begins when our comfortable ideas turn out to be inadequate. — John Dewey

SKILLS: Collaboration

Trust

Use affirmation

WHY: Individuals in groups want to have a sense that their participation is seen by other members as useful, helpful, needed. Students especially want to be accepted. If students feel part of the group, they will perform better.

HOW: Schedule affirmations regularly. Share affirmations when there is occasion for them. Teach students to exchange affirmations as a routine. Make sure everyone who participates knows they are affirmed by the group and the teacher. Don't go overboard, but don't ignore this essential part of collaboration.

3 Skills that Drive the Model

SKILLS: Collaboration

Shared participation

Optimize uniqueness of each student

WHY: Embody Learning is an ideal format for all students to bring their unique strengths to learning. It gives you the opportunity to demonstrate to students that each student has something to offer the group, as well.

HOW: Acknowledge individual strengths, innovations, ideas. Encourage students to listen for new ideas. Be clear about the common standards, and also clear about where unique skills and expression are welcomed.

SKILLS: Collaboration

Shared participation

Invite everyove to sally out of their comfort zones

WHY: Growth, change, and uncertainty can be uncomfortable. Yet learning comes from growth, change, and a break from the routine.

HOW: Acknowledge discomfort. Explain that problem solving, uncertainty, change, growth, and some chaos are a necessary part of the learning and discovery process. For students in stress, assign them to a task with tangible functions — such as taking notes — where they can find some safety. While discomfort is not a goal of Embody Learning, change and growth are built into the model.

3 Skills that Drive the Model

SKILLS: Collaboration

Shared participation

Guide learners to be co-creators of their learning

WHY: In his *Democracy and Education* (1916) John Dewey argues that the type of activities that stimulate real involvement "give pupils something to do, not something to learn; and the doing is of such a nature as to demand thinking, or the intentional noting of connections; learning naturally results."

HOW: Engage students in planning, teaching, decision-making, assessing the learning experience. On a grade-appropriate basis, share the strategic process of putting the lesson activity together. Develop your own style of dialogue. Ask for input.

SKILLS: Collaboration

Shared participation

Ensure shared responsibility for everyone's participation — everyone leads, everyone learns

WHY: If every individual in the group is interested in how the entire group is doing, then "all boats rise." In essence, everyone is a leader.

HOW: A teacher nurtures shared responsibility as a culture with encouragement such as, "is everyone with us, are we all ready, can we help each other…" Give everyone permission to take initiative. Have students get into their work groups when they enter the classroom or at the beginning of a lesson. For each part of the lesson — engage, explore, show — make sure every student is aware of what action to take.

Skills that Drive the Model

SKILLS: Collaboration

Attitude

In working together, set expectations high

WHY: Embody Learning depends on students developing a willingness to work together in learning experiences. And on the teacher's capacity to help students realize how this model aligns with their preferences.

HOW: Let students know how smart they are and how the model plays off their natural abilities to be creative and use their full range of senses and learning capacities. Let them know you will have high expectations of every student, and that they have a great opportunity and responsibility to use their abilities.

> ...Smiling activates the release of neuropeptides ...tiny molecules that allow neurons to communicate. They facilitate release of neurotransmitters dopamine, endorphins, and serotonin. This relaxes your body and lowers your heart rate and blood pressure.
>
> **There's Magic In Your Smile;** *Psychology Today,* Jun. 25, 2015, By Sarah Stevenson

SKILLS: Collaboration

Attitude

Mentor students

WHY: Learning will be accelerated for students, who need to accept you as a mentor and have a guide at a critical moment in their learning. Your role as guide demonstrates a full commitment to teaching at the deepest level.

HOW: Find a resource for how to mentor students at your grade level. Set goals. Set up a pattern of contact. Make a project out of it that has an end date, when you can evaluate plans again. As a mentor:

- be willing to share your experience
- help students identify gaps in their skills
- offer personalized advice
- listen to each student
- help students step out of their individual comfort zones

3 Skills that Drive the Model

SKILLS: Collaboration

Attitude

Be authentic, encouraging

WHY: Teachers who are personable with students get better results. Students sense reticence from a teacher and respond in kind.

HOW: Give students the best you can. Explain the Embody Learning process in which students get to bring their "whole selves" to the learning process. In a grade-appropriate vernacular, explain emotional intelligence and how the entire class can have fun and learn in this process. Establish a vision for that role, true to your values, and work to achieve it.

SKILLS: Collaboration

Attitude

Set high expectations

WHY: Research has shown that teachers expectations can determine students' performance. It is fair to expect teachers to believe that every student has the potential to learn.

HOW: Trust the model and your ability to engage students at a new level. Set what we call *stretch goals* (moving beyond what was previously achieved) and build a new level of achievement for students. Take a goals-approach for each lesson. Help students discover the path they will take toward goals, step by step. Map out steps for reaching goals.

SKILLS: Collaboration

Communication

Establish a standard of information sharing

WHY: If everyone has the same information, everyone is empowered to take action. If it starts to rain and everyone knows how to close the windows, the window will get closed.

HOW: Reinforce instructions. Post or project the lesson content. Assign students to share information with their peers. Make sure that, if students do not have some information, they know where they can get it. Be clear that everyone is a leader and is responsible to either know or ask how things will work. This creates an environment of mutual responsibility.

SKILLS: Collaboration

Communication

Set a protocol for student input

WHY: Student input increases buy-in.

HOW: Establish a habit of getting student input so students make a habit of thinking about how they can provide helpful input. Get ideas from students on how your Embody Learning lessons are engaging students' imaginations. Make sure everyone is participating. Listen and give some response to all input.

SKILLS: Collaboration

Communication

Use deep listening

WHY: If you speak without listening, you are talking to yourself. Listening is where you find out what issues to *speak to*. And listening is where you learn.

HOW: Design listening practice. Ask a student to talk for three minutes while other students listen without talking or asking questions. Then have another student 1) explain what that student heard and 2) ask meaningful questions. Have the class critique the listening and the questions so everyone examines the depth of listening and analyzing for learning that they witnessed. Talk about how to listen. As a speaker who is accommodating good listening, end with a phrase such as "Does that make sense?"

SKILLS: Collaboration

Communication

Model and teach non-verbal communication

WHY: Looks speak volumes. Actions build a profile.

HOW: Being late is communication. Being unprepared, messy, loud when we should be soft, attentive to something important — these all "say" something to someone. The opposite, positive side of these sends messages, as well. A smile is one of the most powerful communicators available to anyone. It's up to us to "have a clue" about everything we communicate and to help students "get a clue." Smile, be on time, wear clean clothes, hold your head up and make eye contact, unfold your arms and be open to other people — these are some basics we can recommend to students and model.

3
Skills
that Drive
the Model

Presentation

Embody Learning is not the first to point out that teachers are performers, holding an audience from the moment school starts until class is dismissed. Some teachers even prefer to "stay in character" whenever they encounter students out of class. Stagecraft has much to offer teachers when seeking to engage students in total commitment learning.

Students take in every aspect of a teacher's performance or presentation. They pick up on the confidence, mood, and even word pronunciations. Embody Learning encourages clarity and conciseness to help students stay focused on learning goals as they engage in a diversity of learning experiences. Body language, use of voice, student's attention, and modeling confidence are the skills we discuss in this section.

> *"The energy level of the audience is the same as the (teacher's). For better...or for worse."*
> — *Andras Baneth*

SKILLS: Presentation

Body Language

Teach with your body

WHY: Students can tell by how you hold your body if you are tired or bored or angry or energized or inspired. Your body, the position of your hands, arms, neck and head, legs and feet combine to send a message, intended or not.

HOW: Be aware of the message your body language brings to students. You are not on stage like a rock star (probably), but you do have an obligation to bring a message of positive energy and readiness to learn. Stand straight, head up, look people in the eye, arms unfolded and feet flat on the ground. Use your body to direct attention to the student who is speaking or toward a new idea, transition to a new subject or instruction for students to move.

SKILLS: Presentation

Body Language

Put your facial expression to use

WHY: Keep in mind your face will be reflected in students'. A smile is generally welcoming, and a scowl is most often threatening unless you are in character or doing comedy.

HOW: Students likely recognize "the look" from parents or other adults, or an attitude being "thrown" by older kids through body language and facial expressions. They may even be able to mimic some looks! Be conscious of what your face is saying even when sound is not coming out of your mouth. Be aware of your resting face — it may have more meaning than you ntend. Decide on the face you need to set the intended tone in your classroom. Keep it authentic but use its power to promote engagement and learning.

SKILLS: Presentation

Use of Voice

Adjust pitch and volume of your voice

WHY: The loudness and pitch — high or low sound — of your voice are primary factors for how well you are heard and understood.

HOW: Get some general assessment of how well your natural voice sounds in a classroom full of students. The quality of sound is called resonance — the depth, which is determined by your physiology. A high pitched voice will get lost in the noise of shuffling papers and student chatter while a lower voice will come through clearer. Support your voice by breathing from the diaphragm — air deep in your tummy, like a singer. Use good posture, whether you speak sitting or standing. Always relax your throat and nasal cavity to increase the reach of your voice. Know the characteristics of your voice so you can adjust volume to be most effective.

> **To put a finer point on volume:** Loudness is an outcome of adjusting our voice to the size of the space in which we are speaking (the actual volume of the space). We adjust our voice to speak more quietly or more loudly so we are heard in the space in which we are speaking. If you and I are on opposite sides of a closet, my volume will be very different than if you and I are standing on opposite ends of a basketball arena. The outcome of adjusting for volume will be expressed in the level of my voice on a loudness scale.

3 Skills that Drive the Model

SKILLS: Presentation

Use of Voice

Play with your voice

WHY: There is nothing like an accent to get the attention of listeners in subjects that have characters in literature and history, for numbers, to animate science and technology.

HOW: This is primarily a bit of fun, remembering that play is critical work in learning. And it will likely be rare. Try on an accent to make a point or get attention to engage students in content. We think in terms of language, but remember dialects from geographic regions of American English — the south, New England, Midwest. Make sure not to mock the subject or any ethnicity. (See video for examples.) Accents are good for removing inhibitions of teachers and students. Make up high tech accents or languages for STEM learning such as coding or math formulas. Get creative.

SKILLS: Presentation

Use of Voice

Enunciate

WHY: It is essential to speak clearly where students have diverse backgrounds and not everyone hears uniformly.

HOW: Speak as though you are modeling the pronunciations of words and sentences. (Note, the last word in that sentence has a T in it. Pronounce it.) Make it your job to *perform* words, sentences and paragraphs for students. Some basic refresher advice on speaking:

- Pronounce all the syllables in a word (as though every word you speak you are pronouncing for a spelling test).
- Pronounce the consonants as though you were playing Hamlet or Lady Macbeth.
- Speak slowly enough that the words can be understood individually.
- Professionals suggest you show your teeth and lift your soft palate, as though you are getting ready to yawn.
- If you are reading, hold the book so your head is up and you are speaking to students and not to the book.
- Put more sound through your mouth than through your nose.
- Pause where appropriate.
- Open your mouth when you speak. Don't mumble.

SKILLS: Presentation

Student (audience) attention

Intensify eye contact

WHY: Dubbed the windows on our souls, eyes are the most captivating of human organs. Fiction gives eyes the powers of romance, deception, and evil. In the classroom, as everywhere, eyes are where people connect with each other.

HOW: Look students in the eyes to affirm your connection with them as a listener or speaker. Suggest students meet the eyes of their peers as well. (The practice of eye contact varies by culture. Look into local cultural customs.) For hesitant students, build trust and invite interaction and consider eye contact the affirmation that trust is being achieved. Think about how the set-up of your room hurts or hinders eye contact and make adjustments — turn to face the presenters. Presenters might wait to begin until they have everyone's attention. When students present to the class, they should make eye contact with students, not the teacher or just one student.

SKILLS: Presentation

Student (audience) attention

Read the audience

WHY: If you can't read your audience — your students — you lose them.

HOW: First, are they asleep, talking with each other, or on their phones? Are they making eye contact with the teacher with facial expressions that mirror the teacher's? Do students respond to content? Read these signs to determine if students are with you. The best remedy for inattention may be a change of pedagogy. Embody Learning leaves no student unengaged with the others and the content.

SKILLS: Presentation

Student (audience) attention

Manipulate interaction

WHY: Not every student has the same level of interaction skills, yet everyone has the potential to learn to be effective in interaction in a collaborative learning setting.

HOW: Despite shyness and inequalities that inhibit some students' interaction, Embody Learning can erase those barriers for most students, be they language, culture, disability, or shyness. Establish interaction goals with students and invite students, at their own pace, to ask questions, ask for help, bring up problems, tell stories (http://blogs.discovermagazine.com/80beats/2010/07/27/study-the-brains-of-storytellers-and-their-listeners-actually-sync-up/) and otherwise be in the conversation. Establish student groups — pairs, quads or other — that rotate so cliques don't form, and have them practice interacting. These skills are critical for learning in collaboration and, of course, for life.

SKILLS: Presentation

Modeling Confidence

Best gift from teachers to students: confidence

WHY: Without uttering a word, teaches can share confidence with students or they can share stress, nervousness, fear. Even if students can't name it, they can feel it.

HOW: Teachers who learn to manage stress or anxiety make a valuable investment for their students. The skill of helping students relax as they are struggling to learn is worth a tidy investment. (We acknowledge stress is a serious issue for teachers. We encourage teachers to pursue whatever assistance they find necessary to relieve the impact of stress on their personal and professional lives.)

3 Skills that Drive the Model

SKILLS: Presentation

Modeling Confidence

Speak clearly, concisely, thoughtfully

WHY: Among everything a teacher does for students, speaking is the most important. It has to be effective for each student.

HOW: Make a mental outline. Speak with intent. Have clear knowledge of content. Start with a "headline." Then don't say more than you need to in order to get your point across. Leave silence after you have made your point. Repeat key points. Practice conciseness. Put content in a simple story if you have the wherewithal. And if you ask a question, let there be silence. Students fill silence with thinking, which is good.

SKILLS: Presentation

Modeling Confidence

Demonstrate transparency

WHY: People who hold in their emotions, keep secrets, or hold back information harm collaboration, cooperation, and teamwork.

HOW: Practice openness. Tell students you want the classroom to be a place where everyone is honest with each other and shares as much information as they are comfortable sharing in order to help each other succeed. Explain that you are their guide for learning and you are also learning. Based on your own personality and teaching style, explain your expectations for them and yourself, and how it feels to be teaching them. The purpose of being transparent is to build a safe learning environment, build trust and expectations. It will develop as students question, test and use the Embody Learning model.

3
Skills
that Drive
the Model

Innovation

If creativity is the generation of new ideas, innovation is the application of ideas, often in a collaborative process. Nobody "makes it" these days without innovation — putting new ideas to work. It's almost a synonym for problem-solving, where we need to use new information in order to resolve issues big or small.

Embody Learning is an innovation, even though many teachers have been using active learning their entire careers. Innovation is sometimes a game-changing technology, but most often it is a great little idea that a teacher devises in the classroom. Innovation is the essential ingredient to good teaching. And it can become a skill that is enhanced with training and goal-oriented practice. Innovation means trying something new, maybe even something new just to you. Those are the same challenges we ask of students. And the challenges we need to make part of our routines.

In this section we explore making creative thinking a habit, developing new perspectives and the role of uncertainty in engaging students.

Learning and innovation go hand in hand. The arrogance of success is to think that what you did yesterday will be sufficient tomorrow.
   - William Pollard

3 Skills that Drive the Model

SKILL: Innovation

Make creative thinking a habit

Give the creative seed to students every day; students will grow new ideas

WHY: If students' creativity is not engaged, students become disengaged.

HOW: Ken Robinson says the industrial revolution model of schools we have now kills the natural creativity that children are born with. Make sure your classroom does not kill natural creativity. Ask students for creative solutions every day. Ask questions differently. When you get a right answer that is not so creative, ask for another perspective. Embody Learning lessons are always creative. Create an environment that invites innovation. Provide examples of creativity. Celebrate innovation.

We have so much to cover and so little time to cover it. Howard Gardner refers to curriculum coverage as

SKILL: Innovation

Make creative thinking a habit

Get cues from students

WHY: From four- and five-year-old preschoolers to 17- and 18-year-old seniors, students have an innate creativity. It changes over their school years, but it awaits the teacher's understanding and access.

HOW: Understand your students as thoroughly as possible. The more you know about students' creative curiosity the better you can build lessons that connect content to learner. In younger years, students' creativity will be accessible to basic content. As students age, develop strategies through discussions, storytelling, building things, media, technology, popular culture. Be curious about student doodles on their notebooks or their smartphone screens. Develop Embody Learning lessons with creative strategies that connect to the students you know well.

the single greatest enemy of understanding. Think instead about ideas to be discovered. — Alfie Kohn

3 Skills that Drive the Model

SKILL: Innovation

Take new perspectives

FIRST: Recognize that every student has a unique point of view

WHY: Students' points of view are assets waiting for teachers to understand and engage as connectors to content and learning.

HOW: Start by observing how students engage with your lessons and each other. Then design exercises in which they express their viewpoint on what is happening in the classroom. And always ask questions, watch, listen and make opportunities for students to reveal their viewpoints.

SKILL: Innovation

Take new perspectives

SECOND: Adjust your point of view

WHY: Make the effort to consider another point of view, or everything you see and do will be limited.

HOW: Wonder how a physicist would teach your lesson on the planets. How a botanist would present photosynthesis. How one of your choice characters from Star Wars, or Wonder Woman, would teach the class. Try things to give you a different perspective. If you usually stand, sit. If you use a handout, use a projector. If you stand in front of the room, stand in the middle of your students. Don't just change to change, but truly seek a different point of view in order to learn something new about what you see from a new vantage point. Be curious.

SKILL: Innovation

Take new perspectives

THIRD: Plan lessons with multiple points of view

WHY: It's your job to try to engage every student in every lesson. The lesson is the basic point of learning — where success or failure for student and teacher is determined.

HOW: Design lessons in which student viewpoints are leveraged as entry points to bring students into the learning experience. In your planning, imagine how the lesson will be experienced from each point of view. Can you design a math lesson for students who believe they don't like math? A civil war lesson from a Native American perspective? Invite students to adjust the lens on a lesson based on their own point of view. Have students learn about other points of view in the classroom and discuss differences. Discuss the challenges, conflicts and issues. More relevant, plan each day's lesson from a different student's point of view. Learn enough about each student to provide the context you need to make the innovation.

SKILL: Innovation

Use surprise to engage students

Turn the unknown into an asset

WHY: Most people like a mystery. Young people stay on Twitter because they can't wait to see what comes up next. The hunt, the pursuit, can be an attraction to learning.

HOW: Use curiosity to draw students into the learning process. Address anxieties students have about uncertainties, change, stress. Explain to students that pursuit is where discoveries can be made.

SKILL: Innovation

Use surprise to engage students

Invite risk-taking

WHY: Humans generally fear failure and consider any action in which failure is possible to be risky. Learning, therefore, must be risky.

HOW: Explain to students that risk-taking is a required part of learning and life. Point out how risk is essential to discovery. Use the stories of the discoveries of penicillin, bioelectromagnetics, trips to outer space and so many others, all of which involved risk and failure. Point out the risks in lessons that ask students to try new techniques, work with content in new ways, take on more responsibility. Talk about how to consider evidence, intuition and trial and error in the learning process.

SKILL: Innovation

Use surprise to engage students

Practice being in the moment

WHY: In a chaotic classroom, every moment holds the opportunity to engage students. Some class schedules include meditation at every grade level. Students' capacities to settle their bodies and minds, to pause and focus, has an impact on academic performance.

HOW: Help students learn resilience and emotional intelligence through breathing, holding energy, and general awareness of the value of mindfulness. Discuss mindfulness in age-appropriate language, and how learning happens in your classroom. If mindfulness is new to you, access the many resources available online (such as https://positivepsychologyprogram.com/mindfulness-for-children-kids-activities/).

3
Skills
that Drive
the Model

Improvisation

Here we look at theater skills, spontaneity, and adaptation.

Hardly a day passes that students don't throw teachers a curve ball, often in the middle of a lesson. Most curve balls are learning opportunities. And many are missed by teachers as they move on with their lessons because they were not prepared to take advantage of the curve ball opportunities.

Improv skills help a teacher prepare for those opportunities to catch the big waves. Teachers use what is called applied improvisation, a term used in design thinking, engineering, sales, technology, social work, medical and health care and so many other fields. Applied improvisation skills show up in presentation and performance, resilience, leadership, and community organizing.

For some teachers, improv is instinctive. For others, it's hard work. But every teacher can learn.

When it rains and you use a garbage bag as a raincoat, you improvise. If you have drummed a spoon on a stainless steel bowl, you improvised. Every time you write a letter or an email, you improvise. You likely know more about improv than you recognize.

> *Improvising is wonderful. But, the thing is that you cannot improvise unless you know what you're doing.*
> *- Christopher Walken*

SKILLS: Improvisation

Theater skills/tools

Expect the unexpected

WHY: The unexpected is going to happen. Being prepared will make it not just tolerable, but productive.

HOW: Change your reflex to the unexpected from panic or confusion to curiosity about the opportunity it presents. Take the challenge head on. Use the stop-pause-think-act method to get your bearings. As always, consider how you can engage students in searching for opportunities in the moment. If you can't come up with something, ask students!

Embody Learning strategy to have handy: *Holding Energy*

Either "freeze" or simply pause; have students do the same. The practice gives everyone the opportunity to stop whatever is happening, to be aware of everyone else, and to focus on what comes next. It works in lessons for just about every subject area at every grade level, as it allows everyone to stop and observe. Use the strategy as a tactic for calming, for changing energy, for stopping a successful process so that everyone can take notice, for stopping an unsuccessful process so that everyone can change direction.

He does it with his hands, by experience, first in play and then through work. The hands are the

SKILLS: Improvisation

Theater skills/tools

Rally your skills

WHY: You are it. In the moment of need, you are the one who has to reach in and find the skill. You need to know what's in the old toolbox.

HOW: Inventory your skills — grace under pressure, ideas ready to pull out of a hat, methods for engaging students to help solve a problem, a fallback Embody Learning engagement strategy. Inventory your skills. It's even helpful to remind yourself, "Oh, this is where I take a deep breath and smile." Highlight the ones that need work. Keep a file of improv ideas. Add an improv exercise to the next teacher professional development session. Design improv style lessons in English, math and social studies for students — have students pull mini assignments out of a hat. Have students throw out questions to each other in various lessons.

instruments of man's intelligence. — *Maria Montessori*

SKILLS: Improvisation

Spontaneity

When there is no fork in the road, go offroad

WHY: The straight road ahead is probably not going to get you to the end of your curriculum pacing calendar — you realistically face many detours and uncharted paths. Also, the human experience of learning is more than intellectual, as we have noted. Spontaneity — used as an asset to learning — can engage the emotional, social and even the physical.

HOW: Swap out old expectations for new ones. Let students make some decisions about how they want to learn, to measure their progress, to work with each other. Create some excitement, mystery, challenge. Be spontaneous regularly, just to optimize opportunities and model the practice. A butterfly flutters in the window and you go with it. Let the butterfly metamorphose into your lesson rather than dismissing the butterfly and directing your class to get "back to work."

SKILLS: Improvisation

Spontaneity

Improvise every day (as if...)

WHY: (as if all teachers don't already improvise every day!) Improvisation engages the attention — and support — of the group. It elicits support from students when you are calculating direction in their presence.

HOW: Use two primary principles of improv to strengthen cohesion among students. 1) Make your scene partners look good and 2) Be positive. In an improv setting where someone is called on to "wing it," everyone is watching, waiting for what will be offered. Stress the supportive nature of improv, where each participant is competitive, trying to out-do the other. At the same time, the team is rooting for each to come up with a great response, so the level of performance continues to rise and the stakes are greater for the next participant. Apply this to academic performance and you have a dynamic engagement tactic.

SKILLS: Improvisation

Spontaneity

Try chaos

WHY: Learning and thinking are not linear processes. Great discoveries come from haphazardness and serendipity. Is it even possible to derive meaning and understanding from a tidy process?

HOW: Classroom management is certainly an objective for the teacher. But management is all in the service of learning. And learning sometimes needs to look like chaos. Expect it. Students are noisy and active by nature. Make sure you enable them to learn by their nature. In the chaos of learning, stop, pause, think and act when you need to. Use the holding energy strategy when you need to. But remember that learning and discovery can be a messy business. If good learning is happening, let it be.

3 Skills that Drive the Model

SKILLS: Improvisation

Adaptation

Make many ideas out of one good strategy

WHY: You might not need many good ideas if you have a few that can be adapted over and over.

HOW: Find the toolbox of strategies, one that fits in your pocket but has many uses. The holding energy strategy, discussed above, may be adapted to many Embody Learning lessons, in many subjects at every grade level. Smart adaption makes the strategy new each time with new content and students taking it in their own direction. One strategy can be the propeller that gets many lessons off the ground and into students' hands. (Note: We suggest you explore many strategies before settling on one or a few evergreen strategies.)

SKILLS: Improvisation

Adaptation

The improv lesson design

WHY: Aren't pop quizzes or teachers questioning students on an assignment like improv? Why not make those same questions on those same subjects an experience students would enjoy and look forward to? Why not make them an improv session? Or a lesson that's all improv?

HOW: Set up the improv session like a performance in which every student has a turn. In preparation, students study content and rehearse questions or formats for improv formats from their peers. Look up some improv games (see appendix on p. 86 for examples from the internet) that can be easily adapted for classroom use. Students develop some questions and the teacher develops some. Allow for funny guesses while the emphasis stays on academic objectives for the lesson. Cheer for success. Teams and individuals can participate. Academic subjects can change each session, or the sessions can focus on the same subject so the class can track progress. Make the session an assessment. Or make it a drill before a test. Use the rules noted above — Be positive. Everyone is rooting for success.

4

Two steps pack the power of Embody Learning

Lesson Planning

"Begin with the end in mind" is the second of the popular *Seven Habits of Highly Effective People* by the late leadership guru Stephen Covey. Covey's statement mirrors a process in manufacturing known as reverse engineering, looking at the process from the end to the beginning to find efficiencies. The universal principle is also expressed in the education planning approach called Understanding By Design which uses a principle called Backward Design – planning by starting with the goal and working backward.

Embody Learning suggests teachers start the lesson development process, with content – the standards.

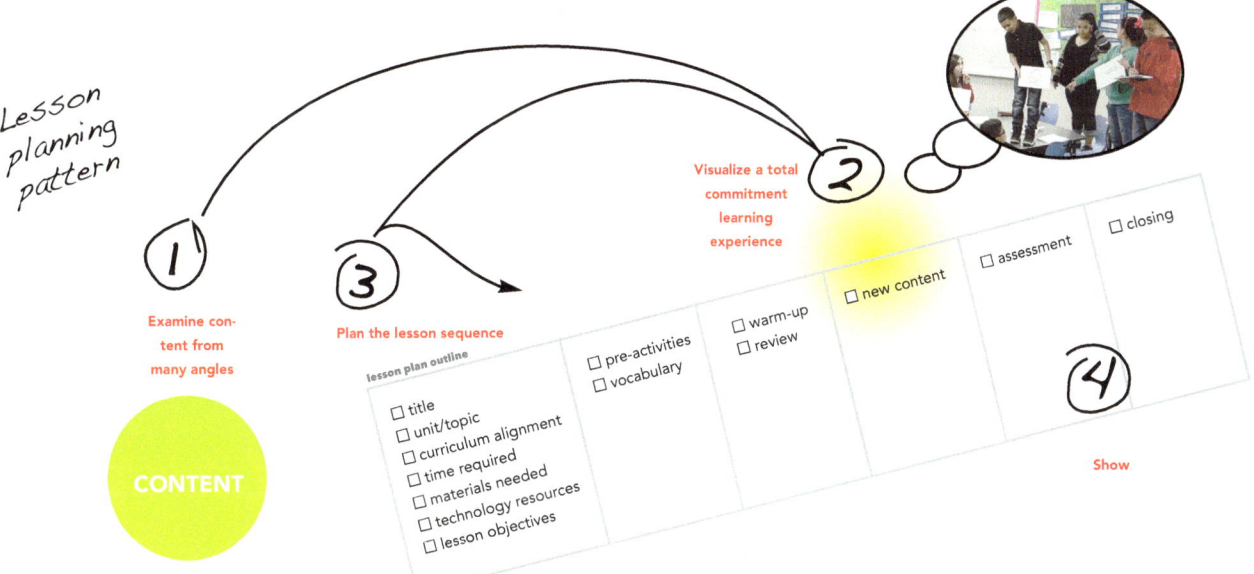

STEP 1, look at content for the clues you need to connect with students. **STEP 2,** put content strategies into the Engage-Explore-Show Embody Learning lesson model.

Then in step 3, continue planning the lesson sequence according to your own lesson planning format. The model fits with any approach or template for lesson planning. Finally, in step 4, show the learning in a demonstration of the lesson, which becomes an assessment.

STEP 1 CONTENT

An Embody Learning lens on content ensures that every lesson connects to students

A teacher's task is to get the content listed in the standards from the printed page into the heads of each student. Well, it's much more than that, as every teacher knows. Unfortunately, in this test-driven age of education, it boils down to getting the content into the brains of students and out of their brains and onto a test, successfully. Yet the greater and much more ethical goal of teaching and education is to impart knowledge and understanding.

For every piece of content that becomes a lesson, it becomes the teacher's task to find the entry point for students; the opening where students make the connection of content to themselves — the relevancy.

Raw content, before it becomes an Embody Learning lesson, has potential — it may be "teeming with living lesson opportunity organisms." Our task is to help teachers see content through a lens in which the life of content shows up; in which the possibilities for active, engaging lessons present themselves. This section is designed to help you take some deeper, wider, second looks at content so your lessons envelop students holistically in authentic learning.

Use your Embody Learning lenses on content to see all the opportunities for student engagement

STEP 1 CONTENT

Look for opportunities inherent in the content

Did I just see that content move?

You might be seeing things. That's good. If you see movement in the content, you can build a lesson in which students embody the movement inherent in the content if that leads them to meaning and understanding.

Adjust your eyes and ears to let content move. If you are multiplying fractions, do you move from top numbers to bottom? When Germany started the Second World War in 1939, did armies move into neighboring countries? If you are spelling cat, cap, and can, is it those final consonants that are moving in and then being kicked out and replaced by another?

Content might also sing, turn blue, bubble, smoke, speak in Latin. If you let it, it will present you with opportunities for engaging students in your classroom. Your task in lesson planning is to discover what is in the content that is begging (or could be coaxed) to be embodied in a lesson.

> **Opportunities for action**: *Where in today's content is the natural opportunity for building an active learning experience?*

You can find linear movement in math, cyclical movement in science, stories and character in literature and social studies, systems and structures in civics and history, emotion and movement in verbs, shapes and other physical forms in nouns, and so on. Approach content with some expectation that content has built-in help for your lesson planning. If it isn't obvious, give it a poke and adjust your creative lenses.

Find an entry point by looking for:

	none				much
movement	1	2	3	4	5
sequence	1	2	3	4	5
circular direction	1	2	3	4	5
linear direction	1	2	3	4	5
puzzle/game	1	2	3	4	5
chaos	1	2	3	4	5
narrative/story	1	2	3	4	5
personification	1	2	3	4	5
symbolization	1	2	3	4	5
compare/contrast	1	2	3	4	5
systems/processes	1	2	3	4	5
cause/effect	1	2	3	4	5
metaphor	1	2	3	4	5
_____	1	2	3	4	5
_____	1	2	3	4	5
_____	1	2	3	4	5

Look for opportunities for engagement in content and rate their potential for use in an active lesson. Customize this list with your own categories. Use it as a lesson planning tool.

As an example, consider the sixth grade math Common Core content below. If you use the form at left, you might rate these categories medium to high:
- movement
- sequence
- linear direction
- puzzle/game
- narrative/story
- compare/contrast
- systems/processes
- cause/effect

Common Core State Standards/GRADE 6/Number streams **Apply and extend previous understandings of multiplication and division to divide fractions by fractions.**
CCSS.MATH.CONTENT.6.NS.A.1
Interpret and compute quotients of fractions, and solve word problems involving division of fractions by fractions, e.g., by using visual fraction models and equations to represent the problem. For example, create a story context for (2/3) ÷ (3/4) and use a visual fraction model to show the quotient; use the relationship between multiplication and division to explain that (2/3) ÷ (3/4) = 8/9 because 3/4 of 8/9 is 2/3. (In general, (a/b) ÷ (c/d) = ad/bc.) How much chocolate will each person get if 3 people share 1/2 lb of chocolate equally? How many 3/4-cup servings are in 2/3 of a cup of yogurt? How wide is a rectangular strip of land with length 3/4 mi and area 1/2 square mi?.

STEP 1 CONTENT

Relevance is essential if you want students involved

The best definition we have found for relevance is from Robin Roberson (2013): the perception that something is interesting and worth knowing.

Rather than something students should or would have a natural interest in knowing, relevance is generally something that students care about. If a student says "So what?", as lesson planners, it's our job to find the answer in our content.

The relevance in the content brings students into the lesson. Once in, students make it their own. They explore and experiment with what it means and how it works. They then become the relevance makers.

> **Relevance.**
> *What in today's content connects specifically to my students?*

Robin Roberson (September 2013), Psychology Teacher Network of the American Psychology Association

RELEVANCE IN LESSONS

Find the aspect of students that connects with the content

- culture
- local community environment
- family member link
- ancestry
- pop culture
- current events/ trends
- career
- geography
- hobby, special interest
- seasonal

culture: food, music, holidays or rituals, styles, fashion

family member link: siblings, grandparents, parents, relatives

pop culture: personalities from the media, music, fashion, TV programs, gaming, concerts, cartoon characters

career: what people do everyday, what students aspire to do, what students talk about (their parents for young students, their plans for older students)

geography: climate, trends in population and human patterns, weather, social shifts, economic shifts that have impact on students, physical changes in the earth, political boundaries

local community environment: clubs, family, organizations that define community

ancestry: immigrants, pioneers, ancestral experiences that are recalled, traditions, language, beliefs

current events/ trends: politics, personalities, news about world and local events, disasters, science trends, technology and medical developments, health

seasonal: the four seasons, by month, according to events that are annual or occur on a schedule (elections, cycles of the moon, etc.)

hobby, special interest: sports, crafts, beliefs, recreation, avocations, collecting, pets, drawing, painting, playing an instrument. etc.

The senses, being the explorers of the world, open the way to knowledge. — Maria Montessori

RELEVANCE IN LESSONS

Define **why** it connects

- personal experience
- aspiration (career goal, bucket list)
- circumstance (event or situation)
- personal passions or interests (music, Pokemon, pets, superheroes, quantum physics, social justice...)
- lesson format options (games, riddles, reading YAF mysteries)

why... because students know it, they live it every day or they remember the experience they had recently and has proven to be effective in engaging students

why... because students already have a deep connection to this passion — a subject or activity — that occupies their time, emotion and intellect... the same real estate in their minds that you are hoping to capture with a lesson

why... because it's an opportunity to piggyback on what is in front of students at the moment, linking our content to real life applications — math to the economy, science to the weather, technology to an election or health newsa or the latest superhero movie release

why... becuase we can develop lessons using a format that studentss already love... gaming format they already play, riddle format they already spend time solving, mystery fiction format they already read at home or during lunch break

RELEVANCE IN LESSONS

Integrate it into the lesson

Put the WHO
and WHY
together and
build a lesson plan.

For example, decide to use a Hispanic (WHO) approach to measuring ingredients for making tamales (creating an experience) for math;
OR
a computer gamer (WHO - career aspiration) persona for developing a system for evacuating a major city (for students involved in recent hurricanes or fires). Each connects WHO and WHY with content objectives in a daily lesson.

RELEVANCE IN LESSONS

During the lesson, continue to shape it

In your planning, include questions that keep students focused on your objectives and a list of key terms...

- ask questions and repeat key words as a reference to lesson objectives
- pause for reflection and adjust direction if needed
- get interim reports from student work groups

see improvisation skills elsewhere in this guide...

learning is teaching, teaching is learning... asking students to explain their learning enables them to "teach" what they are learning, expecially when quizzed for details... after all, what is an assessment but the act of the teacher learning what the learner is learning.

RELEVANCE IN LESSONS

In the end, students will show the connection

As the lesson progresses, students will show how they are personalizing the experience.

For example, as they demonstrate their understanding of the lesson at the end, you can get an assessment of the level of collaboration and commitment each student made to the process. They are also presenting an evaluation of your lesson planning and of how relevant you made the content through the strategy you presented to students.

STEP 1 CONTENT

The senses are natural connections

How does content connect with the senses — taste, sight, touch, smell and hearing?

Most learning comes from using the senses, generally more than one at a time. A multi-sensory experience is a rich learning experience and a realistic goal for every lesson.

The more senses engaged in learning, the deeper the engagement and the more effective the learning (Bransky, 2014). As Judy Willis, a neurologist and classroom teacher, notes, "By stimulating several senses with the information, more brain connections are available when students need to recall that memory later on."

Most lessons engage sight and hearing. Add touch and you remove the lesson from the ordinary. If taste or smell can be part of the lesson, the experience has staying power for learners.

For students who churned butter in second grade, no butter has ever tasted so good on a soda cracker since, no matter how many years have passed.

Bailey, F., & Pransky, K. (2014). Memory at Work in the Classroom: Strategies to Help Underachieving Students: Strategies to Help Underachieving Students. ASCD.

> **The senses.** *What about today's content links to human senses?*

Perceptual systems, particularly smell, connect with memory and emotion centers to enable sensory cues to trigger feelings and memories (Konnikova 2012). The woman who was walking down a busy street, smelled the cherry smoke from a pipe and burst into tears attests to the power of smell on memory. Only later did she connect the smell to her pipe-smoking father who had died only a year before. For lesson planners, senses don't just help students get the content but to also link to relevance of the lessons.

Young learners' senses are especially sensitive to textures. Tactile objects — Play Dough, plush toys, building blocks — can help students grasp basic learning skills like counting and shape recognition for letters and numbers, and focus on tasks. As students become more complex learners, the smell of science kits and sounds of the presidents' voices are the links to facts and meaning.

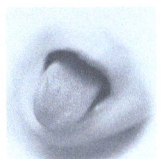   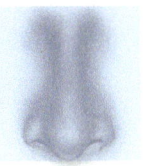 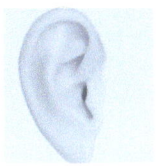

Taste comes from the taste buds on our tongue. Not only can your tongue taste, but it also picks up texture and temperature in your food like creamy, crunchy, hot or dry.

Sight is all dependent upon our eyes. The brain also uses the images from two eyes to create a 3D (three dimensional) image.

Touch is spread through the whole body. Nerve endings in the skin and in other parts of the body send information to the brain. Our skin is the largest organ in our body and contains the most nerve endings.

Our nose is the organ that we use to smell. Our sense of smell is capable of identifying seven types of sensations: camphor, musk, flower, mint, ether, acrid, or putrid. Smell is an aide in the ability to taste.

Our ears, which help us hear, are made of two separate parts: the outer ear and the inner ear.

source: idahoptv.com

Konnikova, M. (2012). Smells like old times. *Scientific American Mind*, 23(1), 58-63.

STEP 1 CONTENT

Students can own their learning

George Washington is so 250 years ago. Algebra is made up of old numbers. The process of photosynthesis has no direct impact on a student's Instagram accounts. So what makes content personal and why would students even want any part of someone else's lessons?

Teachers can take some inspiration that Lin-Manual Miranda managed to make Alexander Hamilton a personal hero to student-age fans of the broadway musical *Hamilton* even after most teachers failed to do the same in classrooms for 200 years. Most of us will not be multi-talented musical geniuses, but we can give students an active learning experience with whatever content we have.

Enrique Feldman, Embody Learning developer, artist and thought leader, tells of a game he played with his teenage son Nick (see Skills videos). He asked Nick each day, "Who are you?" and asked him to notice something new. At first Nick's answers were typical "Aw Dad!," reluctant and mundane. Eventually Nick completely owned the answers

> **Student ownership.** *What does it look like when students work together and demonstrate that they have achieved your goal for this lesson?*

and reframed the question. He reported his personal perspective of the world to his dad every day. The game was designed, like a good lesson, for a takeover. It was offered with patience and wit and, over time, became a guide for Nick to learn to look at the world and develop his own insights.

Teachers can design lessons that transfer ownership to students in the learning process. In Enrique's game, he asked Nick, "Who are you?" Nick changed that question to, "What are you?" so he could describe himself in the various roles he inhabited throughout his school career.

Like Nick, once students get a sense of the learning objective and the content, they can reframe the questions. Of course, they will bring more than a reframed question. Evidence of student ownership will show up in how students embody their understanding and meaning.

When students own lessons using fractions, verbs or great medical discoveries, they can apply their senses and the full range of active learning options. And they may report their experience to their parents:

"I was a flying number when we multiplied fractions."

"I got to be three verbs that revealed the novel in English class."

"We're embodying how penicillin works in chemistry."

4
Two steps pack the power of Embody Learning

STEP 2 ACTION

Build the action into your lesson

Teachers will approach the standards with a vision of students embodying the content in

ENGAGE EXP

People learn by playing, thinking and amazing themselves. They learn while they're laughing at something

Now that you have identified the opportunities in content to engage students, integrate the engage-explore-show imperatives into your lesson plan. Envision students actively embodying content.

engage explore show

active learning experiences (aka lessons) in these three phases.

ORE   SHOW

surprising, and they learn while they're wondering, 'What the heck is this?' — Sandra Dodd

STEP 2 ACTION

Engage

An Embody Learning lesson begins with a phase we call ENGAGE. The model suggests that we engage students immediately, earning full commitment to the learning experience.

The engagement may be physical or verbal. Students may stand and recite a theatrical vocal exercise to get everyone focused when beginning a new lesson, or they may use their bodies to represent content from the prior day's lesson. The engage phase invites all students into the group, almost like gathering before launching in a boat or taking off in a plane. There may be a little chaos as all students practice their roles, gathers their wits, remember what they learned yesterday and prepare for today's content.

A Spanish language tongue twister could start a lesson in Spanish class. Students could form a circle for a gameshow-style math flashcard exercise in middle school. Students might act out verbs they learned yesterday while the rest of the class spells the verbs as they guess them in elementary grades. A high school physics class could arrange itself to illustrate Maxwell's equations. Some teachers use physical warmup exercises from acting classes or vocal warmups from voice lessons.

Education is not an affair of 'telling' and being told, but an active and constructive process.

The teacher sets the level of energy for the lesson in the engage part of the lesson. A demonstration of creativity, openness to exploration, and curiosity sets the direction for students.

The engage phase anticipates the physical, emotional, social and intellectual engagement of the lesson ahead. It prepares students for the challenge of moving beyond their work the previous day.

Logistically, it is a step where students push back the desks and grab the materials they will need.

Students during a warm-up exercise.

STEP 2 ACTION

Explore

The explore phase of an Embody Learning lesson is when students work with new content. They approach it ready to interact, as they would with clay, a box of Legos, a new bicycle that needs assembly, a bus full of rock and roll instruments ready for a group to form a band and go on stage.

Teachers will organize the class in pairs or groups to explore how the math works, what the literature means, what the history event means to the people, what the science does.

Here are some steps for this phase:
- Provide students with the new content (or direct them to content from their reading or research).
- Pose a question, offer a challenge, explain a process for collaborating.
- Share the learning objective. Identify the goal for the lesson. For example, tell students you want to see that they have explored the content and see that they have learned about tectonic plates, volcanoes and earthquakes.
- Provide guidelines for the learning experience, the strategy. These can be detailed or a loose outline, depending on your own students' capacity to manage instructions. Consider those physical, social, emotional and social connections, and think through the four considerations: inherent opportunities in the content, relevance, the senses and how students will own their learning. You might tell students to identify how people feel about the content, to use a globe or atlas, to use personal stories, or to find X number of applications for the content.

- Give students some parameters for the intended demonstration of their lesson. Once students become accustomed to this kind of learning, they will need little guidance. You could, for example, ask for demonstrations for how the solar system works and let them develop their own solutions for demonstrating it in the next phase. Or you could describe what you want to see as an outcome.

A student group engages in formulating knowledge about five chemical reactions.

STEP 2 ACTION
Show

When students show their learning in the third phase of a lesson, it is the ultimate summative assessment. Better than any written test or quiz, a physical demonstration provides the opportunity for students to show in real time the details of the content without the challenges some students face from testing. You can see immediately if students understand the details of the content, learned what was important and why and how it applies to the big idea. You will know if the lesson worked and if the class is ready to move on to tomorrow's lesson.

They show it now, to students and the teacher. Each group may narrate their demonstration or have the rest of the class participate. The demonstration can be simple or elaborate, with props and materials or simulations. It must, however, focus on the learning goal.

During presentations, students may ask questions and make suggestions that enhance the demonstrations, revealing more about class-wide learning. Groups may repeat their demonstrations, stop in the middle and even ask other students to join them. You can optimize this demonstration to learn as much as you can about student learning, and to stimulate continued learning during the demonstration

Some student-developed lesson demonstrations have been repeated classwide and used in test preparation. When Embody Learning students sit for required written tests, it is not unusual to see them physically recalling their demonstrations from lessons.

The greatest sign of success for a teacher... is to be able to say, 'The children are now working as if I

Students demonstrate one of five chemical reactions.

5
Build an Embody Learning Environment

More than the physical layout of the classroom or things we hang on the wall, the environment — some might call it culture — that we build for Embody Learning is a mix of attitude, trust, expectation, energy and receptiveness to experiment and explore.

"We think about the world in all the ways we experience it. We think visually, we think in sound, we think kinesthetically, we think in abstract terms, we think in movement, and in many other ways too. Intelligence is dynamic… and wonderfully interactive." (Robinson, 2006)

Robinson was forecasting the environment in the Embody Learning classroom. So how do we create or build or nurture an environment?

The Embody Learning environment supports active learning, discovery, inquiry, curiosity, wonder and physical expression. Students enter an Embody Learning classroom everyday ready to move, to act: "Where are we going today? What action are we taking? What experience are we having?" Creating such an environment in which students' expectations are high is the ultimate goal for building student engagement. Students come to class ready for total commitment learning.

Here are four tools for shaping an Embody Learning classroom environment.

Robinson, K. (2009). *The element: How finding your passion changes everything.* Penguin.

1 - Checklist of factors shaping classroom environment

☐ Design the physical classroom to accommodate active learning, classroom routines, content support, and that stimulate student interest and curiosity (some Embody Learning elementary classrooms don't have desks, but use tables and some chairs that leave a large space open for most lessons.)

☐ Attitude — the goal of Embody Learning is that everybody is in. Be constructive/positive, focus on an optimistic, can-do approach to problems and tasks, encourage efforts from every student. Encourage students at every level.

☐ High expectations — in an Embody Learning environment, expectations cover how students engage in the daily process, not just what they achieve at the end. High expectations challenge all students to support a team environment even among individuals with varying abilities.

☐ Be fair — The integrity of an Embody Learning environment means the teacher needs to set the standard, be the adult, and see that every student not only gets a fair shot at succeeding, but actually does succeed. That means, to the degree possible, helping each student as much as each student needs help so all can succeed.

☐ Bring parents into the mix as much as possible. Because Embody Learning puts learning in such stark display, classroom visits from parents or demonstrations for parents are always enlightening for them.

☐ Teach respect as an attitude (address bullying, anti-bias education, community building strategies, if appropriate) and clarify expectations of how students treat each other (resiliency, issue resolution, trust, social skills). With Embody Learning depending on effective collaboration, civil interaction is essential.

☐ Recognize good choices (even risks, big efforts, hard work, failures that result in learning, as well as successes).

but what great teachers also do is mentor, stimulate, provoke, engage. — Ken Robinson

2 - Reflective practice checklist

Reflective practice is as critical to continual improvement in Embody Learning as it is for any pedagogy. This is the set of reflective questions we use in training and coaching. Modify to fit your needs.

- ☐ How did the environment support learning? How can it improve?
- ☐ Was the Embody Learning strategy an effective match for the learning goal? What was the evidence?
- ☐ What specific factors promoted student engagement?
- ☐ List student-initiated ideas that came up during the lesson.
- ☐ How did the strategy enable students'– critical thinking skills?
- ☐ What evidence do we have that students are learning?

3 - Evaluate how students are interacting with content in the Embody Learning environment.

- ☐ Students actively demonstrate clear understanding of the academic standard(s) through accurate representations of content.
- ☐ Student innovations of the original task clearly align with the lesson objective and academic standard.
- ☐ Student innovations of the original task clearly and appropriately apply the content learning to a new or different context.

Teaching means creating situations where structures can be discovered. — *Jean Piaget*

4 - Evaluate individual student engagement in the Embody Learning environment.

☐ The student is highly motivated and engaged throughout the learning process.

☐ The student explores and initiates ideas that demonstrate clear motivation to understand and extend new content learning.

☐ The student demonstrates proficient use of inquiry and higher order thinking skills through Embody Learning strategies.

☐ The student demonstrates leadership in collaborating with peers to seek new ways to solve problems, represent learning, ask questions, look for evidence, and provide constructive feedback.

☐ The student improvises with existing structures and content throughout the learning process as a means for seeking, exploring, and representing new ideas.

What teachers say

Teachers tell us they are forever changed by the teaching practice of Embody Learning. Once teachers adapt Embody Learning methodologies, they realize the student engagement benefits immediately. Here is what teachers say.

"Embody Learning provokes more critical thinking, making connections across curriculum, and activating various parts of the brain."

"It results in a passion for creative thinking."

"Students will understand concrete concepts more easily and they will have fun doing it."

"Embody Learning will have a huge impact on deepening understanding in all areas of learning. It's a way to help students see transfer of key knowledge/skills across subject areas."

"It allows kids to discover through trial and error, not right or wrong."

"Children will take a wider range of thinking and problem solving skills on to adulthood."

"Once I began using Embody Learning, students began to take ownership for the words that they presented. They were more fully engaged and took pride in their work as it was something they had to perform in front of the whole class. As we used more Embody Learning strategies students connected mathematical processes to vocabulary they had worked with months earlier."

"I have rethought and redesigned final exams in College Algebra so that the students will do their finals through performance, not on paper. The students had to use their bodies to represent the Pythagorean Theorem (very enjoyable and funny). I will be doing this as often as possible in all classes! Working with Embody Learning was a transformative experience!"

Appendix

IMPROV EXERCISES PULLED FROM THE INTERNET

Old School

A nice verbal and impulse warm-up that lets students flex their rap muscles.

RULES:

Students stand in a circle, and begin by letting out a Beastie Boys-style intro (students might need to listen to a few BB songs to get the hang of the rhythm): "Ba da da da da da da da da! Ba da da da da da da da da!"

A player initiates with a verse, for example, "Woke up in the morning and I went to school," (All: "Ba da da da da da da da da!")

The player to his/her left then rhymes a new verse: "But first I took a dive in my swimming pool." (All: "Ba da da da da da da da da!")

Play continues around the circle, with players rhyming to the first verse.

If a player slips up, then the intro happens again, and the offending player starts a new rhyme.

Play continues until you win a Grammy (or as long as you want).

So I'll (exercise)

This exercise forces listening and gets players taking smaller, more logical steps with their story building. It also helps players when they draw a blank in a performance setting. The first player makes any kind of statement. For instance, "It is a lovely day out." The next player in the line says, "WHAT YOU ARE SAYING IS THAT--It is a lovely day out, SO I WILL--go for a walk." The goal is to say the next most logical thing in the story. The next player would say "WHAT YOU ARE SAYING IS THAT--I'll go for a walk, SO I WILL--get my shoes." The story that builds should be a logical one. It will not be a story that will win Pulitzer prizes, but it will make sense.

Word At A Time (exercise)

Each player in the circle contributes a word into the story. If the first person to speak says "Johnny" the next person could say, "set", the next person would say "out". And so on. This is the most commonly used of all the improv exercises.

Yes And (exercise)

In Yes And the players are constantly saying, 'yes and'. The mechanism goes something like this. One player may start off with, "Your coat is so lovely." The response of the other player could be, "YES AND I made it for you." The other player responds, "YES AND I have a thousand dollars for it." "YES AND I am going to use that money to make a hundred more coats for you." The players must always have the 'yes and' at the beginning of their sentence. This seems contrived and it is. It is remarkable how much easier it is to notice players that insist on controlling the scene. They cannot bring themselves to accept the offer. The most common response is, "yes and but."

Alphabet Scene (game)

The actors must build a scene within 26 starts. Most places allow for more than one sentence to follow the first sentence. When this is done, it is important that actors really punch the word that starts with the letter. Activity is important as it allows the scene to progress independent of words. This game ceases to be a challenge rapidly.

Backwards Scene (game)

The actors start with an ending to a story. Then each actor must ask herself what would have happened immediately before this event and then portrays the most likely thing that would have preceded. Actors will find themselves frequently asking themselves, "she just said...so I would have..." Very hard stuff. Keep it very simple and never talk in the future tense, that already has happened!!

Conducted Story (exercise)

The goal of the conducted story is to have the players tell a story that moves seamlessly from one player to another. The goal of the conductor is to make the story flow as well as possible. If the conductor moves from one player to another, the new player that is speaking must continue on as though there were no pause. For instance, moves from player "A" who said, "Many children were afraid of Carl for he was known to ha.." to player "B", who would continue seamlessly "..ve piles of library books that were overdue." The key is listening. It is a listening exercise. The four players that are not speaking must be listening. They all must have the next word ready to go, and only if they are listening will that word make any sense. The players must also be accepting of what is happening in the story. Forcing their own agenda will show up quickly. Words like, 'but' and 'instead of' reflect someone who denies another players' offers.

In Sync

For this game you will need to come up with three things that can be easily mimicked with hand gestures. For example if you picked a king, the sign could be to use your hands to form a crown above your head. If you picked a chicken, the sign could be to bob your head and cluck. You can pick anything, just make sure all the players know the three things agreed upon and what their signs are. At your signal, each player will pick one of the three things and will make the appropriate sign. The game continues until everyone in the group picks the same thing to act out. It is fun to watch who leads the group in which thing to act out and who is stubborn in following!

Group Mime

This last game involves group coordination to mime a group activity. For example tug-o-war, rowing a boat, peddling a 10-person bike, etc. This game encourages suggestions from the audience and team work from the players. If there is no audience, then simply ask any one of the players for a suggestion of what to mime.

SOURCES:
https://funattic.com/improv-games/
http://improv.ca/whooshwhoa/

www.ingramcontent.com/pod-product-compliance
Lightning Source LLC
Chambersburg PA
CBHW041124070526
44584CB00003B/272